Loving your doubt

First published in 2022

ISBN 9798431905407

The right of Adrian Ashton to be identified as the author of this work has been asserted in accordance with sections 77 and 78 of the Copyright, Designs and Patents Act 1988.

Contents

Introduction

Just writing the words makes me doubt I should go any further – but I must: too many people won't let me walk away from this after I've talked about it for so long. Well, not talking about imposter syndrome per se, but rather how frustrated I get about all the 'experts' who are presented to us to speak on the subject who, to me, seem to me to be missing the point about it (*or rather, several points*). And when I explain what I think the reasons are for this to those same people, they all say I should be doing something like this: writing it all up.

But let's start with why I have imposter syndrome in writing this (*despite all the encouragements I've had from different people who think otherwise*): I don't hold any clever qualification in psychology or sociology; I don't work in a charity that helps people rebuild self-esteem and confidence in themselves after traumatic effects.

I'm just a person with what seems like a lot of life experience when I compare my story to others', and who tries to think about things critically and constructively. And as a result, from time to time I seem to come up with ideas and suggestions that people find helpful. Today, those ideas and suggestions are around imposter syndrome, and why I think (*nearly*) everything you've heard and have been told about it is (probably) wrong.

But who are you, to be reading this?

Chances are, if you're reading this, you're one of two types of people:

1) Someone who is worried that they might be struggling with imposter syndrome, and wants to get a better handle on how they approach their work. In which case, you're probably already reading posts in Facebook groups, and think-pieces in various websites' features pages.

   I too, read lots of those things, and I think that in part there's always something relevant and pertinent in them. But I'm also concerned that they're one-sided or don't help you fully engage with the ideas, hence this deeper reflection that is this pocket-book.

OR

2) You're someone who writes those posts and features on websites about imposter syndrome. And if so, you may recognise some of the ideas in here that you've also shared over the years. That isn't meant as a confession of plagiarism on my part – rather, a validation that most of what we actually think we know and understand about imposter syndrome is quite widespread and has been for some time. All I'm doing with this pocket-book is drawing all these strands of it together in a single place, in hopes that

it will help us all make better sense of how we think about ourselves and approach our work.

But you may not be either of the above – you may be someone who's researching into workplace behaviours; someone who's looking for future careers advice; or maybe you're my mum!

Whoever you are, my hope is that you'll find content in this that isn't just of interest, but more importantly, is of practical application.

Are you a freelancer? (don't worry if you're not!)

But before we dig into the whole syndrome itself, I wanted to pause to reflect on whom it's most likely to affect, or who'll struggle with it.

Although we can all be prone to it, regardless of our profession or employment status, it's freelancers and the self-employed (*like me*) who seem to struggle with it the most. That's based on threads and posts in discussion forums, conversations with management teams and HR people, and such like (*including research from Freelance Heroes which found that over 90% of us suffer with imposter syndrome*).

But I have a thought that this isn't actually the true case.

My thought is that it's freelancers who are more likely to be open about it than our employed counterparts:

- As freelancers, it gets lonely. And the gremlins of self-doubt can start to circle around us very quickly without recourse to conversations with our peers about our concerns. As such, the freelancer discussion forums are littered with people questioning their value (*based on what they feel they can charge clients, and how far they believe they can lead the relationship with them*).
- As salaried employees, we're more likely to be part of a team with whom we can mutually bolster our ego and sense of ability all the time. We also seem to

have common workplace cultures that don't make it easy for people to admit that they may be struggling or feel able to ask for help (*more on that in the sections to come...*).

- And (*as will be picked up in later sections*), most of the writing and research to date around imposter syndrome is focused on people in employed roles.

Defining it for the purposes of this pocket-book

Let's use Wikipedia's entry as at 14th Dec 2020 (which when I started writing this pocket book):

Impostor syndrome (also known as impostor phenomenon, impostorism, fraud syndrome or the impostor experience) is a psychological pattern in which an individual doubts their skills, talents or accomplishments and has a persistent internalized fear of being exposed as a "fraud". Despite external evidence of their competence, those experiencing this phenomenon remain convinced that they are frauds, and do not deserve all they have achieved. Individuals with impostorism incorrectly attribute their success to luck, or interpret it as a result of deceiving others into thinking they are more intelligent than they perceive themselves to be.

And let's also use the mug-shot of my face on the cover too – there's the face we have that other people see (*calm, confident, and such like*), and then there's our face as we see it (*nervous, unsure, anxious about getting 'caught out', because we're out of our depth with regards to whatever it is we find ourselves involved with*).

Maybe it's not a weakness – but a superpower?

Everything I hear and read about imposter syndrome seems to start with an implicit assumption that it's a bad thing, and we should get rid of it (*and by association, there's something wrong with us because we're struggling with it...*)

So, the first challenge in re-thinking our relationship with imposter syndrome is to re-set this starting point – DON'T AUTOMATICALLY ASSUME IT'S A BAD THING!

Look at the FTSE100 – it's referenced by governments, investors, banks, policymakers, and others as the standard by which we draw confidence in the economy. But look closer, and you'll see that these top100 companies are constantly changing. One day they're the best in the country, and then suddenly they're not.

What causes a business to lose favour in the eyes of its customers; what causes it to lose the confidence of its backers? There are probably many reasons, but I suspect we could trace them all back in some way to people becoming complacent.

And complacency is a problem – it means we don't recognise risks for what they really might be, it means we overlook opportunities as they don't seem immediately relevant to us; it means that our competitors start to overtake us; it means we start to become less credible and relevant to our customers and others as the world continues to change around us at ever-increasing speeds...

One of the key features of imposter syndrome is that it means you doubt that your skills and experiences are what they should be – which should force us to (re)invest in ourselves, seek out new experiences, and ultimately be even better at what we do. Without this element of self-doubt, how far would we really take such 'CPD[11]' seriously, in making sure it was the right type, and creating the best results for us in our work?

And at the other end of the analogy scale is the boorish manager that we've all known at least one of – the person who seems to revel in taking any and every opportunity to share with those around them (*usually in meetings or at networking events*) just how great they believe they are, all the brilliant stuff they believe they've achieved in and for their organisation, and why they deserve your unconditional adulation (*or so it seems…*). And then think about how that person made you feel, especially about the prospect of working with them.

However right or wrong it may be, imposter syndrome forces us to appear modest and unassuming – putting us in a position where we feel the other person knows more than

---

[11] *For clarification, I've always had two definitions of the ubiquitous 'CPD' tag: the traditional "Continuing Professional Development", and my more enjoyed "Convivial Procrastinated Drinking" which sees me peer reflect with my counterparts in a pub…*

we do, so we default to inviting them to initially lead the conversations. The other party usually then takes that as a sign of interest and respect, meaning that you can more quickly establish a more positive working collaboration. And all because imposter syndrome stopped you believing your own hype.

Imposter syndrome can also help us avoid making mistakes that we wish we hadn't. It can act as a failsafe in making us pause and double-check: is this a risk I really feel qualified to take?

There's a story about a bank robber that came to inspire what's become known as the Dunning-Kruger effect. In the 1990s a man robbed a bank, having smeared lemon juice on his face as he believed this would make his features unrecognisable to the staff and security cameras (*lemon juice is the basis for homemade invisible ink*). His confidence far exceeded his competence. It seems like a funny story in the retelling, but it's a salutary reminder that we shouldn't always act on our first instinct and belief without some form of external sense-checking.

There are plenty of mantras out there about 'feeling the fear and doing it anyway' (J.F.D.I.; and similar), but it never hurts to sometimes have that moment where our brain asks us 'are we really sure we're not going to overstretch ourselves on this one?'. Surely it's better to renegotiate expectations, than find yourself flailing in a job or contract that damages your credibility and reputation?

OK, maybe it can be a problem…

However, I'm not naïve enough to think that, with a few carefully(ish) crafted paragraphs, I can change your mind about imposter syndrome and that you now welcome it with open arms, wondering why you ever wanted to rid yourself of it at all…

And there's good reason why it's usually touted as a problem: it causes us to doubt ourselves.

Self-doubt, unless carefully managed, means we find ourselves trapped by a paralysis of uncertainty over how we should act – after all, if we don't have confidence in our skills and abilities, how can we be sure that we'll do the right thing in how we act?

Without confidence in ourselves, we also don't tend to put ourselves forward or volunteer for experiences and activities that might otherwise enrich our lives and those of others around us.

Not believing we really are up to the job we're being asked to do, or we're "faking it until we make it", means that we'll also always never fully commit to anything.

Imposter syndrome robs us of our confidence in ourselves, sometimes to a level where this self-doubt starts to exceed our actual levels of competencies, skills, knowledge, and expertise.

And all of this ultimately leads us to living lives that are less fulfilled - and can start to generate more stress, anxiety, and in some instances - medical-grade depression.

However, it's easy to assume that when it happens, it happens in a certain way. Except it doesn't. As I'll explore later in this pocket book, just as imposter syndrome can be rooted in different causes, the way it manifests can also present different experiences for different people:

- We don't volunteer, or put ourselves forward for new opportunities within our teams or organisations amongst people we know;
- We don't apply for that dream job or placement that would mean a change in our working lives or living circumstances that would place us amongst people we don't yet know;
- When we're approached by others with invitations and offers of jobs, contracts, or similar, we default to saying "no".

Nearly all of the above examples have something in common – other people suggesting or recognising we may be more than we think - or believe we are.

Imposter Syndrome can tend to force us to focus on where we are now, and where we've been. But people around us tend to focus on what they see as our potential: what we might be capable of in the future, and where we might be able to go, based on what they've seen us achieve in the past.

This is a crucial point about imposter syndrome that's often overlooked or not even recognised when we usually talk about it: Imposter syndrome tricks us into focussing on our past, when we need to spend equal time and energy in trying to think about and imagine what our futures might be – especially as the people around us are focussed mostly on that part of us.

If we're not careful, this dichotomy in how we view ourselves and how others view us, can not only lead to our missing out on experiences that might otherwise offer us more excitement and 'warm and fuzzies', but it can also mean that our relationships with others around us start to suffer and break-down because we're not engaging with each other from the same starting points about who we are, and who we're seen to be.

What does the science say?

Perversely, the research about imposter syndrome suggests that the more successful and skilled we become, the more we're more likely to experience it, (*which is a sign that it can be harnessed as a 'super-power' in keeping us sharp in these high functioning roles and positions*).

But, at some point, nearly all of us will experience Imposter Syndrome in our lives, regardless of role, professional, or position in life. A paper in the International Journal of Behavioural Science referenced by Time magazine identified that 70% of us will be so afflicted, regardless of role or circumstance.

Research also shows that Imposter Syndrome can be sparked by our internalising a sense that we're not meeting the expectations that society or others have on us (*and how many of us challenge such expectations, and how many simply accept because" I'm just a woman / temp / unqualified / etc"*).

I'm also aware that, for some people, Imposter Syndrome has its origins in a wider political societal agenda of patriarchy: its 'discovery' in the 1970s (*see the next chapter*) also coincided with a time when women were starting to gain more senior roles that were previously held by men. Some would therefore argue that in seeking to undermine one's belief and confidence in oneself, imposter syndrome is a manufactured mechanism that is impressed mainly upon women, in order for men to more easily retain the management and senior roles that they have traditionally held.

It's always been with us

Imposter Syndrome didn't officially didn't exist before 1978 because that's when the first writing about it appeared from psychologists Pauline Clance and Suzanne Imes. Also, initially, it was reported as only affecting women.

However, long before 1978, Albert Einstein once said of himself: *"The exaggerated esteem in which my lifework is held makes me very ill at ease. I feel compelled to think of myself as an involuntary swindler."*

Thankfully, since that original paper in 1978 we've rethought it. Hence why this pocket book is hopefully pertinent: helping to continue to keep challenging our assumptions about imposter syndrome, and make sure that we best understand (*and respond to*) it.

It doesn't just apply to the workplace

Up to this point, this pocket book, like most other things I've come across relating to imposter syndrome, has made a HUGE implied assumption. That imposter syndrome only applies in the context of workplaces.

Except it doesn't.

It happens whenever we do anything that brings us into contact with other people, in any context or setting: parenting, being a sibling, hanging out with friends, and such like.

And that's because there will always be other people who know more than we do about everything. BUT those people won't always be in the same places you are. So, why are we living in the shadows we perceive them to be casting over us when they're not even here with us?

"It must be me because everyone else thinks this session brilliant, but I think it's a waste of time…?"

Increasingly, I seem to find myself in events and group calls where a speaker is introduced, whose message and delivery everyone fawns over. But I'm left sitting there, thinking "yes, and…?".

I'm left feeling that I've just wasted an hour, an afternoon, a day, a weekend that I'll never get back. And I'm of an age where I'm starting to realise just how important how I spend my time is… (*some of you will understand what I'm referring to – for those of you who don't, give it a few years then re-read this bit*).

And my imposter syndrome's first response to this feeling is: "it must be because you're stupid if you didn't hear or see what everyone else obviously did!". Or, "if you didn't think this was relevant to you, why did you book onto it in the first place – don't you even know what you need or what's important to you?".

All of which gets jumbled up together in our heads, and leads us to feel more confused and upset than we did before…

But what if it isn't us and it also isn't the other people, at the same time (*in a weird Schrodinger's cat, quantum mechanics kind of way*)?

We all have different life experiences, stories, and insights we've gathered over the years of our lives. And they're all different to everyone else's. And they mean that we all know things that everyone else doesn't.

And my idea in relation to this is that I've been self-employed for the best part of 20 years at the time of drafting this pocket book. Before that, I was employed in business support agencies which saw me invited to influence policy at the Bank of England and help inform government plans. Prior to that, I was a student placement in one of the UK's top100 marketing agencies. And lots more stuff in-between.

I've also worked my way through a divorce; tried to support and encourage my parents as best I could after my father came within hours of death for different illnesses that no-one can understand how he was able to walk around with for so long; been through a few rounds of counselling as part of my professional practice, and fulfilled a promise to my kids to do snow angels for them whilst wearing nothing but a mankini...

And this leads me to my idea that a lot of the other published content 'out there' is aimed at people who are in the first phases of setting up their own businesses, or in the first years of being freelance, when everything's new and scary. I'm past that stage, and have already explored the themes and content they're introducing. So, why should it engage me as much as it does them?

I, and everyone else, in these sessions is right to feel that it's either been a waste or brilliant according to our life experience – and we're all absolutely right.

But despite this, my imposter syndrome keeps dragging me back into these webinars and events for fear that things are changing about how we understand issues or new research and models that are being created, and I don't want to start risk becoming complacent...

Ways it manifests and originates

So far, this has (*hopefully*) all been interesting, and there have been points at which you've found yourself wondering how it is that I could know about your own experiences to have echoed them back to you as I have (*spoiler alert: it's called empathy*).

But this pocket book isn't just about exploring why we need to stop seeing imposter syndrome as a foe to be vanquished, and in doing so we can somehow magically start loving life more. It's also supposed to be practically useful also, rather than just another stirring motivational TED-X type talk. (*You know; the ones we all rave about but - within a couple of days or even hours - struggle to articulate any specific action we've begun to enact or adopt in ourselves from what they taught us*).

And for some of you reading this, you're now thinking that this is where I start to list strategies and actions you can adopt to fully harness the potential of your imposter syndrome.

Sorry to disappoint, but we're not there yet.

Another idea I have which is critical to our understanding about imposter syndrome, is that so much advice that's offered around it is bland and generic. It doesn't actually help you do anything tangibly useful.

And that's because it's not tailored to you – it's based on generalities. But I think that our imposter syndromes all originated in, and affects us in, different ways. So why should we assume that the same approaches will be equally valid for everyone?

If you were feeling unwell, and went to the Doctor, you wouldn't expect that they'd hand over a prescription without asking what exactly it is that you're feeling unwell with – the analogy being that you wouldn't treat a broken arm in the same way you would the measles (*yet both cause pain, upset, and debilitate us, albeit in different ways*).

As has been explored earlier in this pocket book, imposter syndrome manifests in different ways in how we act in response to it. And if it's stopping us from putting ourselves forward in some situations but not others, then surely, we need to best understand what triggering it in us. Because if we can better understand the cause, we have a better chance of finding the best ways to manage resolving it. For example, we might be the life and soul of our team, but despite encouragements by them, would never dream of accepting roles that would offer more leadership opportunities; but think nothing of applying for similar roles in other organisations. So, we need to ask what specifically triggers the imposter syndrome in our team environment.

The following section outlines, in brief, some of the experiences we might have at different times in our lives that might start to sow the seeds of imposter syndrome in us. The preceding chart to this list serves to illustrate that Imposter Syndrome can be rooted or 'grown' in a variety of circumstances – ranging from our childhood (the life we've known, and our personal self) to possible future careers (the life we don't yet know and the professional self we're yet to become):

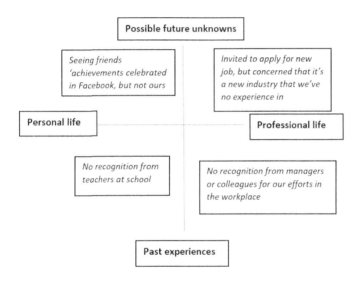

Possible 'origin stories' of our feelings of imposter syndrome

So, what's your imposter syndrome rooted in?

- Perhaps as a child, our parents had high expectations of us, and we've carried some of that into our adult lives: feeling that we're failing and letting others down if we're anything other than perfect;

- Perhaps we've been in abusive relationships, were someone else behaved in ways that belittled us and meant we constantly questioned ourselves, even when we're doing the right things. Such learned behaviours can be hard to break, even if we manage to remove ourselves from those relationships;

- Perhaps it's because in our workplaces, managers and others have never offered or given us recognition for our achievements. But they did to others, which left us feeling that our best wasn't good enough;

- Or perversely, maybe it's because we've found ourselves accepting roles and tasks when invited to by others that we feel wholly unqualified and lacking the skills for, because the person/people who put us there didn't take the time to spell out to us exactly why they felt they had the confidence in us to be able to fly in those positions?

- As a society, we're bombarded with messages and expectations that we'll all have exciting careers, achieve academic success, raise the perfect family, enjoy at least 2 holidays overseas each year and always have a car that's no more than 5 years old... For many of us, that's simply physically not achievable within the laws of this universe. But because we don't achieve these things, we feel we've failed, and are therefore a fraud;

- We may have recently become part of a new community, work team, or such like: as such, we don't really know anyone, or how things work here, and yet everyone else seems to. As the newcomer we don't want to appear stupid by asking what we might think are silly or obvious questions. Yet here we are, thinking ourselves unqualified to be here because we don't know how this new world is supposed to work when everyone else already does...

- And as crazy as it may initially sound, there may also be a cause that's related to our trying to be professional and non-judgemental: In the context of paid work or project contracts, while it's important to have a sense of what the final outcome of the activity should be in guiding and managing it, we should always try and be open-minded to these outcomes, and the processes we intend to use, not being the right ones as we progress and learn more. But this can mean that if we don't have certainty in how we're approaching the work or relationship, then we lose confidence that we can actually be the right person to be there, which feeds back into the imposter syndrome loop...

Strategies to manage / harness it

So – it's now that part where we share some approaches and ideas on how you can start to think about managing your Imposter Syndrome. They're offered in no particular order, nor grouped by any logic: because as most of us who've experienced Imposter Syndrome know, Imposter Syndrome doesn't usually act in a rational, ordered way...

The following section outlines in brief, some of the approaches we might adopt at different times in our lives that may help us better manage, and even benefit from, our imposter syndrome. Preceding it is a simple framework that shows how different ideas may be more or less relevant to our circumstances, and how when we might plan to try and enact them:

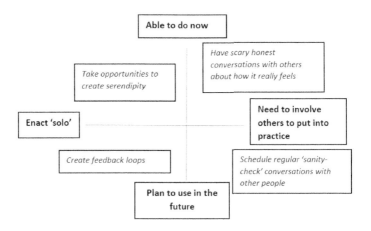

Possible ways to approach managing feeling of imposter syndrome

- Accept that there will always be someone better than you. But they're usually not here, you are. So, act now, otherwise, you'll never do anything, and nothing will change for the rest of us.

- "But if I get it wrong, people will laugh at me" – this may be true, but they'll be laughing at someone else tomorrow…

- Think about what fear means for you. Perhaps you can re-interpret fear as a sign of strength. You may, for example, be sensible to placing importance on the issues and experiences you're facing, and taking them seriously.

- Create feedback loops (*that you create for yourself in recording the encouragements, recognitions, and validations you receive; and that others can offer you, as reminders to keep challenging self-limiting beliefs you may be holding about yourself*). These can act as positive reinforcements, but if you find yourself starting to ask for them too often, you may be risking drifting too far the other way, and into narcissism.

- **Don't** 'fake it till you make it' (*a common encouragement*) – if you're already doubting that you're good enough, then unless you've won awards for your acting, how can you be sure you'll be able to bluff others? Doing so will likely only put more pressure on yourself while you do this...

- Try and widen the perspectives you expose yourself to in how you reference and relate to your feedback. After all, a goldfish will probably think it doesn't have any great skills until a mouse falls into its tank with it, and through this new contrast realises that its ability to swim and breathe underwater are actually pretty impressive after all.

- Try and seek moments of serendipity[2]. For example – when I chance tweeted a glib comment at a conference which Ed Mayo was chairing, it led to him inviting me to the pub for a drink to quiz me over my ideas that might help him better develop strategies to lead a national movement. Similarly, the extension of an outrageous invitation to the Ernesto Sirolli (*or so it felt to my Imposter Syndrome at the time*), led to his inviting me to share a zoom call with him to hear some of my stories and experiences, to help him better refine the approaches he uses with communities around the world.

---

[2] *If you don't recognise the names in this section, feel free to Google them, and then you'll hopefully appreciate why I felt these were such important examples to include in this pocket book*

- Don't read this pocket book (*or anything else*) as 'the ultimate answer' – our understanding about everything changes over time. The science about imposter syndrome in the 1970s originally said that it only affected women in certain roles! We therefore should be constantly reviewing and challenging our ideas and understanding[3].

- Check the time and place you're in when you feel imposter syndrome starting to creep up in you.

    o Every case study I ever read that's presented as good and inspirational practice is usually based on something that worked because of a specific set of people, that were in a certain place that offered particular circumstances, and at a time when things were available/could happen in ways. All of these things are usually very hard to easily photocopy to where we are now. Recognise that what's needed in one context won't be needed universally every time. It's ok to be 'good enough' (*and having lived and worked*

---

[3] *In this context, my 'reframing' of this pocket book in this way - offering it as part of a wider and ongoing conversation, helps to reduce the pressure on me (and it) to be absolutely perfect. It can therefore BE imperfect, and could be, and should be, and will be – so syndrome reduced!*

through floods, pandemics, and such like, being 'good enough' is actually a pretty impressive achievement!)

- Never in the history of worrying about something, has someone saying "try not to worry about it" ever worked. It's ok to give that person a slap if they try and say it to you.

- Try and accept that it's OK to be you – we live in a society where, (*through the media, social media, performance appraisals in workplaces, sometimes disjointed family relationships, the advertising tactics used by companies, and such like*), we're increasingly encouraged to compare our experiences and achievements to other peoples'. But what worked for them, and why, (*remember that earlier point about 'best practice case studies'*), probably won't for you. And try to remember that that's OK, – because where those people are trying to get to in their lives is different to where you want to get to. What's most important to them will be different to what's most important to you.

  - We're all different people (*"Infinite Diversity in Infinite Combinations", as the Vulcans of Star Trek would say; or if you're not a Trekker/Trekkie, remember that not everyone likes Marmite*). It's ok to be impressed by others, and to be inspired by them – but it's not ok to try and be them, and then beat ourselves up when we fail (*because we're not them*).

- Being British can be a problem: there's something in our culture that makes it almost impossible to admit that we're struggling *("stiff upper lip, and all that!")*. But if we can, and we can do it with others that may also be struggling with imposter syndrome, then that sudden ability to fully accept and recognise that we're not the only ones dealing with these feelings immediately assures us that we're not alone in our self-doubt.

- As hard as it can be (*again, for a combination of those reasons in which our imposter syndrome can be rooted*), try and accept that it's OK not to be perfect in everything – and that sometimes, "good enough for now", or even just showing up, is a far bigger accomplishment and achievement than we might otherwise allow ourselves to think[4].

---

[4] *When I started writing this pocket-book, the world was in the midst of a global pandemic, and just getting up each morning, putting on clean underwear, and feeding the dog (being "good enough for today") was enough, And, more than that, it was accepted by everyone that that's the most we should expect of each*

- Try and avoid aiming for 'the next thing' that will help you conquer imposter syndrome. For example: *"if I can win this promotion, then that will prove I really am good enough and assure me that I don't need to doubt myself anymore"* – but it will likely only refresh your imposter syndrome, as this new role will come with new responsibilities and worries that you didn't have before, and restart the cycle of thinking that you're not good enough, and if only you can get that next qualification or promotion, that will resolve it...

- As I've argued earlier, there's can also be something quite important about not getting rid of our imposter syndrome: it's part of 'the human condition'. Research tells us that nearly all of us will experience it at some point in our lives. So, trying to rid ourselves of it completely would also mean getting rid of some part of what it means to be human...

- Ultimately, be patient. Everything takes time - including gaining the skills, knowledge, and experience you'll need to objectively prove to others and yourself that you are qualified. If this were an illness, there's no magic pill that a doctor could give you that would immediately resolve whatever your

other and ourselves in such crises.

ailment was. So why do we think we can magic imposter syndrome away with a few positive thoughts? Try and take comfort that every expert out there was once as you were, and until you get to where you want to be, you have your competencies: your gut instincts and intuition. They've gotten you this far, so surely they're worth sticking with for now? And, remember: to be considered 'professional' is usually about your competencies and behaviours – not your knowledge or experience.

Of the above, some may seem pertinent to you, some too abstract, and others way out of what you're able to do. But all of them may seem a little impersonal in contrast to the earlier sections of this pocket book: the part where I reflected on what it was that brought me to this point of drafting these ideas, researches, and suggestions together for you.

So, with that in mind, there are a further schedule of strategies and ideas that I'd like to share which are things that I've personally adopted and found useful in helping me manage/harness my own imposter syndrome over the years:

1) Being a scientist.

Sadly, not the sort that brews fantastic concoctions in secret labs with lots of futuristic equipment, explosions that are nearly big enough to be of concern but are mainly just the test tubes and beakers showing off, and machines that go 'ping' randomly. I mean the sort that uses the 'scientific method': gathering evidence and data to create understanding and introduce change.

Other people may seem more qualified than us because of their position, age, and such like – but their understanding, knowledge, and skill is based on what they're read and whom they've spoken with. We all read different things, and speak with different people to each other all the time, which means that sometimes we may miss something – something that could be potentially quite important, but which everyone else doesn't seem to have spotted.

To illustrate this point: in years gone by, the UK government introduced a new legal form for social enterprises called the Community Interest Company to much aplomb and hurrah in that sector. I was sceptical because I read up on what the rules and laws that regulated it would mean for businesses who adopted this form. I felt that there were some causes for concern layered within these, but all of the sector bodies I tried to speak with about this appeared to me to be dismissive of what I was trying to voice and explore. And I wasn't seeking to score points against anyone here – my interest was for the benefit of future social enterprises, so that if they chose to adopt this form, it wouldn't 'trip them up' inadvertently.

As this legal form was also introduced as part of a wider policy for the sector from the government of the day, it's perhaps unsurprising that many didn't feel they could or should query it – after all, it was part of a wider raft of things happening for the sector that people were keen to see happen.

And who was I to question it? I had (and still don't) no formal legal qualification to offer me any credibility or basis to lobby company legislation with. I wasn't part of any recognised campaigning or lobbying body. But I had the evidence and research to support my concerns – and on the basis of presenting my arguments using these alone, the regulator conceded that changes to the form should be made, and they subsequently were, despite the form originally being overseen by expertly qualified and experienced solicitors, barristers, and others who are steeped in how company law works. In their rush, they'd missed something that I hadn't, because we'd each spoken with different people and read different things before we'd acted in our respective roles.

2) Not being Batman

As a sole trader, I've adopted a range of practices in how I work which apparently go far beyond what most consultants, freelancers, and companies do (based on feedback I've had from peers and standards setting bodies). This pocket book isn't the place for me to delve into them all, but there is one that I think is especially pertinent to the themes of imposter syndrome: being able to understand and accept how other people really see us.

When I fell into freelancing, I was aware that there would be things I 'lost' – one of which is regular line management and formal appraisals which would usually serve to help me better reflect on how I was doing in my job and what I might focus on in the future. In not being an employee, I lost access to this practice, so sought to replace it with others: one of which is an adapted 360-degree feedback.

Every couple of years, I randomly select clients I've worked with, people I've collaborated with, and others whom I've networked with, and ask them a single question. Each time, it's a different question, but its purpose is to try and provoke and elicit their views and experiences more honestly than they might otherwise accidentally fall into, where I to share more of a traditional survey or feedback sheet.

To date these questions have included:

- *What's my superpower?* (sadly, no-one ever says I'm Batman...)
- *What's my kryptonite?* (which is always interesting, as no-one ever says I'm weaker in areas that I might think I am)
- *How might you introduce me?*

Over the years, I've collated what people have kindly taken the time to share back with me, and reflected on it in posts on my blog. Every time I do this, I'm surprised that their experience of working with me always indicates that they think I'm better than I think I am.

Having these regular feedback loops is one of the ways I've found most powerful and useful in managing my Imposter Syndrome.

3) We're all Michelangelo (the renaissance sculptor, not the ninja Turtle)

There's a story about Michelangelo who, when approached by a young boy to ask to be his apprentice, asked "why?". The child apparently replied that he thought Michelangelo was the finest sculptor in the world, and wanted to learn how to make statues as beautiful as he did. To which Michelangelo replied: "I can't teach you that – because the sculptures are already in the stone; all I know how to do is to remove the bits that aren't needed to reveal them."

I've been delivering training and learning programmes, as informal brief sessions through to accredited programmes with universities, for decades and feedback from learners and participants consistently shows I'm delivering at higher standards than people are used to engaging with. Even so, I still sometimes find myself wondering "am I really good enough to be teaching the stuff I do?". And that's when I think about Michelangelo – heralded in his own lifetime as a genius, yet seemingly not sure exactly how he managed to achieve what he did. And it's that approach that I've adapted as the basis for how I approach any learning or training I deliver: as human beings, our brains are always doing far more than we realise all the time and we know far more about more things than we often realise. I don't see my role as being the expert tutor (*although I've various pieces of paper and such that can offer people assurances as to this status if they'd like*) – rather, what I'm doing is helping people actively realise and embrace what they already knew, but usually didn't think themselves good enough for what they needed to know. In effect, many people on learning and training workshops and courses are also struggling with imposter syndrome at some level!

4) Always listen to the Doctor, and know where your emergency exits are (or, be more like Eddie Izzard)

I'm not ashamed to admit to being a whovian (with an equal love for both the original and rebooted series), and I've often taken inspiration and example from that show in my personal and professional life.

Perhaps one of the strongest examples of this in relation to Imposter Syndrome is an episode of the 'new-Who', "Forest of the dead[5]" (Warning! Spoiler alerts imminent). In one scene, the Doctor appears to be trapped in the middle of a corridor (*with nowhere to run*), his companions lost so unable to save him, separated from the TARDIS, and the aliens bent on killing him are closing in on all sides. "Surely", we thought, "this is it. There's no possible way he can escape to run another day."

When suddenly he asks the oncoming creatures, *"don't you want to know my secret before you kill me? Don't you want*

---

[5] http://www.drwhoguide.com/who_tv39.htm

to know how it is after all these years of adventures and battles, I've always managed to survive every seemingly impossible encounter?". Of course, at this, the creatures pause – as do we as the audience. At which point, the sonic screwdriver starts to buzz, and he cries *"I never let myself get into a situation without knowing that there's a way out"* (or words to that effect). And a trap door suddenly opens underneath him, allowing a helter-skelter ride to another part of the complex he's been trapped in.

Some would argue that this is lazy storytelling on the writers' part – but I think there's something here in how we might hold and manage our imposter syndrome. Imposter syndrome causes us fear: *"what if it goes wrong?; what if it doesn't work?"*; and such like. If we can create a 'back door' to be able to 'escape' through before we enter that situation, then that part of the imposter syndrome is able to be negated, as we'll know what we can do if that worst case eventuality really does occur.

It's also a practice I've seen used by Eddie Izzard in many of their stand-up shows. As a free-wheeling performer, Eddie is famous for shows that are, in effect, a stream of improvised consciousness. And sometimes that means the jokes don't always hit the mark with the audience. But they know this, and if you ever watch Eddie when this happens, you'll see that they have a few 'go to' responses that they whip out to deliver which allows the audience to know that Eddie's realised it's gone wrong, to easily draw a line under that attempted gag, and to restart afresh. Those little tricks mean that they're more confident to be braver and try new things

41

because they know how to recover themselves quickly if things start to go wrong.

5) Brush our teeth more regularly

All of us know and agree that brushing our teeth twice a day is really important – yet it's also something that, if we're honest, we don't particularly look forward to. But somehow, we manage to (mostly) stick to this routine, mundane task every day.

Why? Easy – because when we were younger, our parents encouraged (nagged) us to develop brushing our teeth as a habit.

And it's building habits that can be another powerful way to start to better manage our imposter syndrome. Trying to set a regular schedule of either reviewing feedback we've received about ourselves, having a 'sense-check' conversation with a trusted colleague, or any of the other practices that we see and hear regularly shared when imposter syndrome is being discussed.

These strategies and mechanisms only work if we use them – and we'll only use them if we're in the habit of using them. And the bad news about habits is that they take time to build up if we're going to be able to sustain them. There are, however, few 'quick fixes' when it comes to approaching how we manage our respective imposter syndrome.

Going back over the above list, it seems that most of what's in there is common sense (*a surprisingly rare superpower*), or rallying cries you'll have heard or read elsewhere. And that's because a lot of how we feel and manage Imposter Syndrome, can actually sometimes be that straightforward (*a bit like accounts and bookkeeping – once you get the basic principles, they're actually quite straightforward and many people then wonder why accountants make it seem like such a dark magic and use the strange phrases they do...*).

But none of them will work by themselves. Remember that our imposter syndrome will be rooted in different things for each of us, and the circumstances and lives we live will all cause us to respond to those influences in different ways. Going back to my analogy about seeing the doctor if you're not feeling well: some people are allergic to different medicines, so what will treat one person won't be right for another. Likewise with imposter syndrome – each of our imposter syndromes are unique to us. Our challenge (*if we choose to accept it)*, is to figure out if we want to ditch it or keep it; what it might be rooted in; and what practices will best work for us (*likely through trial and error, I'm afraid).*

Ultimately, if we can find ways to become more comfortable and accepting about who we are as shiny, fluffy, beautiful people, we can become more confident in our abilities and how we engage with the people and circumstances we find around us. And perhaps a useful way to start this is to (re)define what success means for you in this life: stop striving to achieve the things that wider society and others suggest you should be aiming for, and think about what makes you happy instead. After all, it's your life, no-one else's, and you have to live with it, not them.

So, what now?

This is it, we're almost at the end of our tour of Imposter syndrome. Hopefully, there's been something here that's given you pause to reflect on what you may have held as beliefs and assumptions about it, but at the very least, you now feel more informed about how imposter syndrome might be affecting you.

And you now have a choice (*I don't write things for people just to read, but to provoke...*):

1) You can actively choose to do nothing about your Imposter Syndrome

This is absolutely fine – it's what most people do, so you're probably in good company. After all, it's your life, not mine, that you're living; and it's only you who has to sleep with your conscience at night (*or whenever it is you choose not to be awake*).

But I would caution and remind you, if you're taking this path, remember that imposter syndrome limits our beliefs about ourselves. It means that we don't think we're good enough to jump at opportunities as we stumble across them (*and more than this, you'll probably not be looking for them*), and that means we've missed the chance for a new adventure; to learn something new about ourselves; to meet new people; to try out new things. Ultimately, it may mean less of a life through missed potential. However, you may feel that the cost of chasing that potential is too high for you. And if that's the case, then you should be open about that and encourage others to stop pushing you in ways that may be right for them, but aren't for you.

2) You can actively choose to start to try and do something with your imposter syndrome

This is the flip-side of the above: challenging our self-limiting beliefs about ourselves can instil a refreshed confidence and renewed excitement about trying new things and becoming part of adventures that we might never have imagined. And some of these won't work out, and we'll risk making mistakes and have people laugh at us. The prospect of that starts to fire up our imposter syndrome. But if we're actively managing those feelings, recognising them for what they are, then we have a better chance of being more than we currently are.

Whichever option you choose – try not to be ashamed or fearful when you feel the hand of imposter syndrome might be on your shoulder, and it starts to whisper in your ear. Being scared at the prospect of doing something is ultimately a good thing. Fear reminds us that we're alive. Fear triggers our bodies to start to pump adrenaline and other hormones and chemicals around our bodies and brains, and these cause our senses to be heightened (if we allow them to). –So, for a short period, imposter syndrome can actually make us more superpowered than we usually are!

And now, the bad news (which actually isn't that bad after all)

Imposter syndrome isn't something that will ever completely go away, however well we recognise and manage it, but - as I've argued - that's OK. In fact, it's more than OK, because we need our imposter syndrome in order to help us keep our edge, remain grounded, and ultimately be part of helping each of us to be the best type of human we can be.

Thank you list

Tony Robinson – he name-checked me 3 times in his book, The Happipreneur, so I feel I should reciprocate by mentioning him at least once in this

Mike Bull – he's similarly referenced me in academic research papers he's published about people who've influenced the development of the social enterprise movement in the UK, so here's my attempt at paying that back

Matthew Bellringer – for inviting me to be a guest on his 'Delightful Dissent' youtube/podcast series, which (*as well as some saying saw me acting 'slightly' unprofessionally on it*), helped provoked some of the ideas that have formed parts of this pocket-book

Ed Goodman – for founding Freelance Heroes, the peer community for freelancers. Each year it stages #FreelanceHeroesDay, which includes conferences and webinars – and it was that event in 2020 that acted as the catalyst for me to start writing this

Various national policymakers and legislators (*probably best for me not to name you publicly*) – despite my not holding any formal qualifications that should entitle me to, for letting me influence national policy and instigate changes to legislative acts on the basis of my own views and understandings of issues derived from research, evidence, the lived experiences of people I've worked alongside

My kids (Edward, Henry, and Winter) – for never doubting my ability as a parent to always try and manage to do the right thing

My mum and dad – for their ongoing encouragement and cheerleading

Zoe – for waiting over 30 years for me to finally recognise what I should have done when we were both teenagers

Neil Tenant and Chris Lowe – for writing the soundtracks

Eddie Reader, for the lyrics to 'What you do with what you've got'

Monty Python, for the machine that goes 'ping'

Tash Morgan-Etty of Write Rabbit for helping me avoid spelling mistakes, and for ninja turtles

Bibliography

The below is a schedule of materials I've looked up, reflected on, been inspired by, or simply been part of a pile I created through 'blind' google searches[6]. It's not intended to be comprehensive or complete, but an indication that I haven't just come at this from what's in my own head, but thought about my own positions and ideas through the lens' of others who've come/written before me on this subject:

"I wore the Juice" – the Dunning-Kruger Effect; Little, Brown and Company's medium blog, Jun 14, 2016

Professionalism – meeting the standards that matter; Mind Tools' website, Feb 2021

Impostor syndrome – facing fears of inadequacy and self-doubt; Mind Tools' website, Dec 2020

Overcoming impostor syndrome as a leader; Nokukhanya Mchunu writing for the Common Purpose blog series; 12 Aug 2020

Impostor Syndrome; Wikipedia; (as at 14 Dec 2020)

---

[6] I wanted to try and avoid bringing any bias or prejudice to the selection of source and reference materials, so took all the results that search engines generated at face value without filtering them before accessing them.

5 different types of impostor syndrome (and 5 ways to battle each one); Melody J Wilding writing for The Muse blog in 2020

Impostor Syndrome, a reparative history; Dana Simmons of the University of California; published in Engaging Science, Technology, and Society vol 2 (2016) p106-127

What is imposter syndrome?; Arlin Cuncis writing for the Very Well Mind Website in May 2020

The Clace Imposter Test scale; published as part of The Imposter Phenomenon: when success makes you feel like a failure, by P R Clance, 185

Feel lie a fraud? Kirsten Weir writing for the American Psychological Association website in Nov 2013

Five top tips from Freelance Heroes Day; Helen Deakin writing for the Freelance Heroes blog in 2020

How to kick self-doubt to the curb and become your biggest cheerleader; Sarah Townsend writing on her blog in Nov 2020

Imposter Syndrome: the truth about feeling like a fake; Katherine M Caflisch writing in Aug 2020

Yes, Impostor Syndrome is real. Here's how to deal with it; Abigail Abrams writing in Time Magazine in June 2018

Printed in Great Britain
by Amazon

79253722R00031